How to Draw Monster Reptiles

A Step-by-Step How to Draw Book

Published by Top That! Publishing plc
Tide Mill Way, Woodbridge, Suffolk, IP12 1AP, UK
www.topthatpublishing.com
0 2 4 6 8 9 7 5 3 1
Printed and bound in China

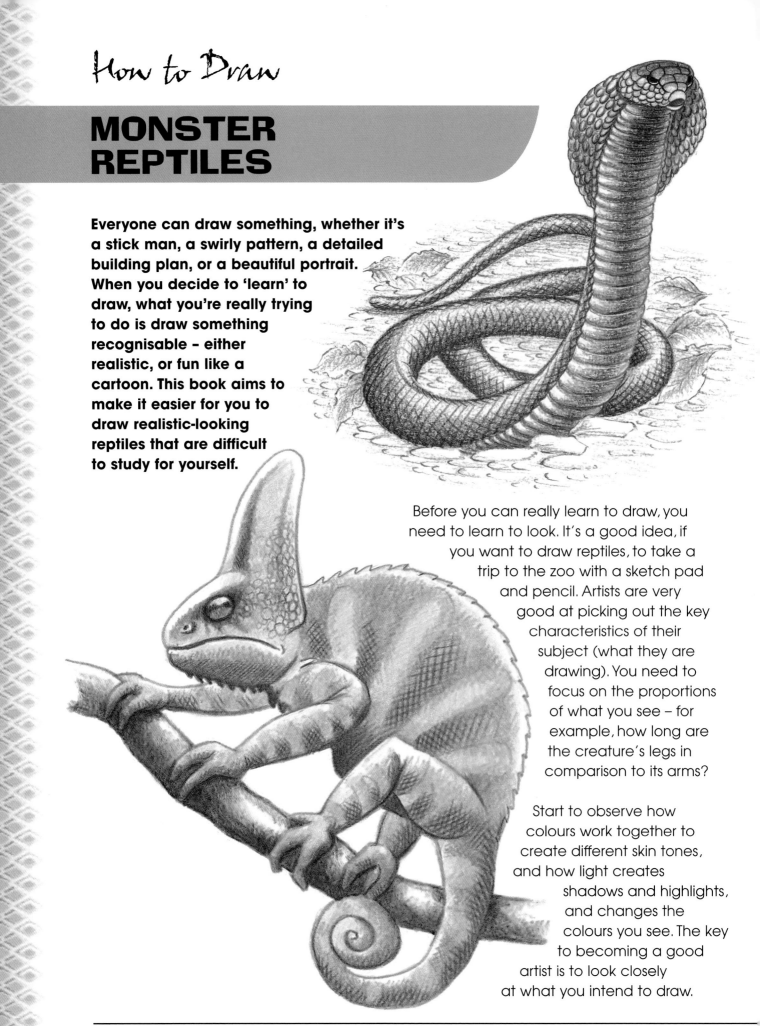

How to Draw

MONSTER REPTILES

Everyone can draw something, whether it's a stick man, a swirly pattern, a detailed building plan, or a beautiful portrait. When you decide to 'learn' to draw, what you're really trying to do is draw something recognisable – either realistic, or fun like a cartoon. This book aims to make it easier for you to draw realistic-looking reptiles that are difficult to study for yourself.

Before you can really learn to draw, you need to learn to look. It's a good idea, if you want to draw reptiles, to take a trip to the zoo with a sketch pad and pencil. Artists are very good at picking out the key characteristics of their subject (what they are drawing). You need to focus on the proportions of what you see – for example, how long are the creature's legs in comparison to its arms?

Start to observe how colours work together to create different skin tones, and how light creates shadows and highlights, and changes the colours you see. The key to becoming a good artist is to look closely at what you intend to draw.

How to Draw

BASIC TOOLS

PENCILS

Drawing pencils are made up of a wooden case surrounding a graphite stick in the centre, which is what makes a mark on your paper. The graphite is mixed with clay; the more clay, the 'harder' the pencil. There should be letters on your pencil to tell you how it will draw. H stands for hard, and 2H or 3H and so on means they're harder still. These pencils leave less graphite on the paper, making a line which is lighter in tone. A letter B tells you how black the line will be (sometimes referred to as the softness of the pencil). Again, 2B or 3B means the pencil is even softer. A letter F tells you the pencil can be sharpened to a very fine point.

For your drawings in this book, it's best to have a selection of pencils. Try H, HB and 3B to start with. Draw soft outlines with your 3B, fill in more detail with the HB, and finish off after you've added colour by highlighting tiny details (eyes, nostrils and so on) with the H pencil.

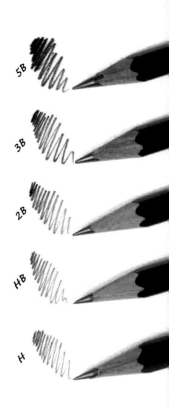

PAPER

Make sure you buy a sketch pad that isn't too big (you'll waste lots of white space around the edges and it's harder to carry everywhere you go). Try to find paper that's white, instead of cream, and not very see-through if you hold a sheet up to the light. Unless you're going to use watercolours as well as coloured pencils, you shouldn't need expensive textured art paper.

SHARPENERS AND ERASERS

You'll need a pencil sharpener, of course, but to get a very fine point on your pencil you'll also need sandpaper. The easiest way to do this is to borrow a nail file from an adult! There are lots of fancy erasers in the shops, but you want a plain-coloured artist's eraser. (The novelty ones in bright colours are no use for drawing.) You might also need a putty rubber which can be moulded into shape to shade areas of your drawing – good quality sticky putty works well for this.

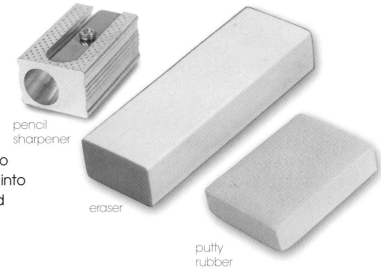

pencil
sharpener

eraser

putty
rubber

How to Draw

BASIC TECHNIQUES

This section explores some of the basic techniques you will need to develop if you are to successfully draw the reptiles in this book. Becoming familiar with your pencils and discovering what tones they create and what they should be used for is central to becoming a good artist. Learn to be versatile, how to draw lightly and how to add strong details and shading. Also, learn to see your subjects differently, break them down into shapes and study their proportions.

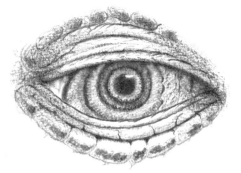

USING YOUR PENCILS

Below is an example of how to use your pencils to create a realistic-looking turtle's eye. Mastering the techniques required for this activity, which include drawing a soft outline, adding detail, shading and highlights, will set you in good stead for the rest of the book.

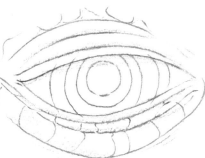

1 *Use a soft pencil, such as a 3B, to lightly draw the basic outlines of the turtle's eye, as shown.*

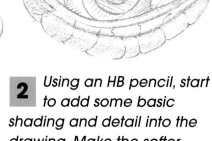

2 *Using an HB pencil, start to add some basic shading and detail into the drawing. Make the softer outlines darker and use the same technique to add depth to the lines between the scales and shadow to the underside of the upper eyelid.*

3 *Continue to add depth to the drawing with further shading using a 2B pencil and for the darkest parts a 3B pencil. Notice where light reflects from the eye and use a rubber to create white highlights in these places. Look how the eraser has been used very delicately to create a glint of light on the pupil – it is details like this that bring the drawing to life.*

It's very easy to shade an area of your drawing and then accidentally smudge it with your hand. One way to avoid this is to put a piece of paper under your hand whilst you draw.

SHADING TECHNIQUES

Don't be scared to shade using your harder pencils. Just remember that harder pencil tones can't be rubbed out in the same way as your light pencil marks if you make a mistake. Practise shading with different types of pencil and study other people's drawings – you'll see that they often use several different tones to create shadows instead of just black.

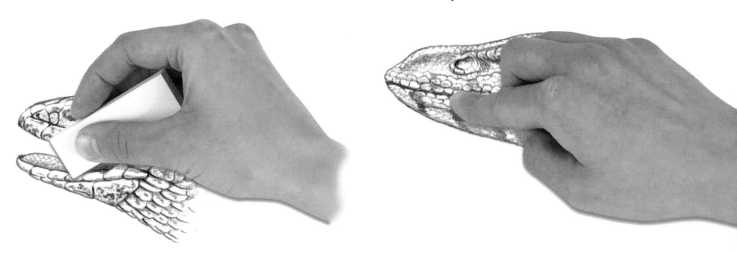

Use your fingertip to smudge areas for a very soft effect. Your putty rubber can be used to lift pencil marks right off the page. Keep one corner of your ordinary eraser very sharp and angled so that you can use it like a pencil point. This can be used to add white or pale highlights.

USING SHAPES

As you read this book you'll learn to see how creatures are made up of basic shapes. When you study an animal, check out all the proportions involved. Is its tail half the length of its body, or twice as long? Draw in these shapes and proportions very faintly at first so you can change them if necessary.

How to Draw

COLOURING EFFECTS

This section shows you how to develop colouring techniques you will use throughout the book, and how to really bring your drawings to life. Colouring pencils can be used to create realistic-looking tones, shadows and highlights. Learning to blend several colours together will provide you with a wonderful way of capturing the true nature of reptilian skin and the subtle shades within it.

APPLYING COLOUR

It is best to use ordinary colouring pencils to get to grips with the drawing techniques introduced in this book. Begin by studying your chosen creature, or a photograph of it. Look carefully at how many different colours and shades give it the overall effect.

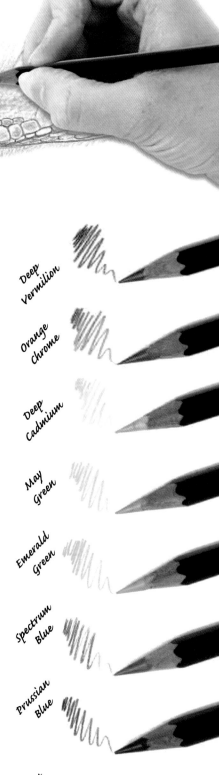

Deep Vermilion

Orange Chrome

Deep Cadmium

May Green

Emerald Green

Spectrum Blue

Prussian Blue

Light Violet

Imperial Purple

1 *Your first colour should be the lightest shade you see on the reptile. Colour gently and evenly wherever you need the colour. Don't forget to miss areas if you need white highlights, or very dark areas with no pale shades.*

2 *Now gradually add darker colours to the drawing. These will start to form the shapes and contours of the creature's skin, scales and limbs. Details such as these will be the last thing you add to your picture.*

BLENDING COLOURS

You'll have to learn to study your subjects very carefully to get realistic colours. Many reptile skin tones have lots of subtle shades within them. You'll see that there's a huge difference between a lizard with green skin and yellow highlights, and one with green skin with brown highlights. Many greens have a blue quality to them, while some are warmer, even with hints of red. The colour chart (right) should give you a good idea of which colours blend together to create certain shades.

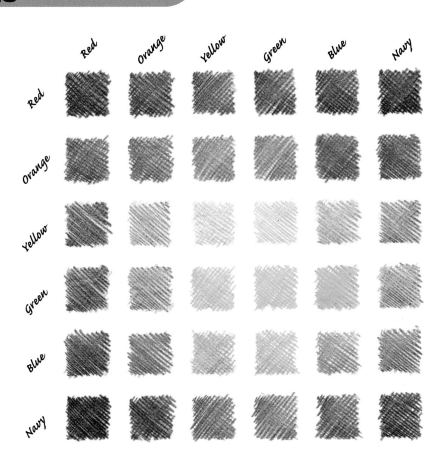

SHADOW AND LIGHT

After drawing the basic outline, look at your subject to see which parts are in shadow and which have the light falling on them. Shadows and highlights are easy to see in real life, but more difficult to capture on paper.

Highlights should be a paler version of the basic colour. Don't just leave an area white – remove some colour with your eraser to leave a hint of what was there. Add yellow, pink or turquoise to give a warm, or cold, effect.

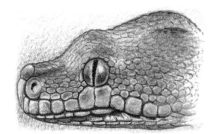

Shadows should be built up carefully, adding more and more colour to the right areas. Think about how the light is being blocked to cast the shadow. Look carefully at how tones change, and skin folds, to add shadows in the right areas.

How to Draw

KOMODO DRAGON

With an average weight of about 70 kg, komodo dragons are the world's heaviest lizard. They have a long body, well-developed legs, and a deeply forked tongue, which they flick out as they search for food. Komodo dragons have good eyesight, but they find most of their food by tasting the air with their tongue.

Where do they live?

Komodo dragons are restricted to the Indonesian islands of Komodo, Rinca, Gili Motang and Flores. These arid, volcanic islands have steep slopes and little available water for most of the year.

1 *Start by lightly drawing the creature's outline with a 3B pencil. Draw the head, neck and body of the komodo dragon and simply indicate where the legs and tail come out of the body. Rub out any mistakes and make sure that you get the proportions right.*

2 Rub away construction lines that aren't needed and flesh out the creature a little. Add the eye to the picture and 'cut' the head in two to show the top and bottom jaws. Indicate a forked tongue at the front of the mouth.

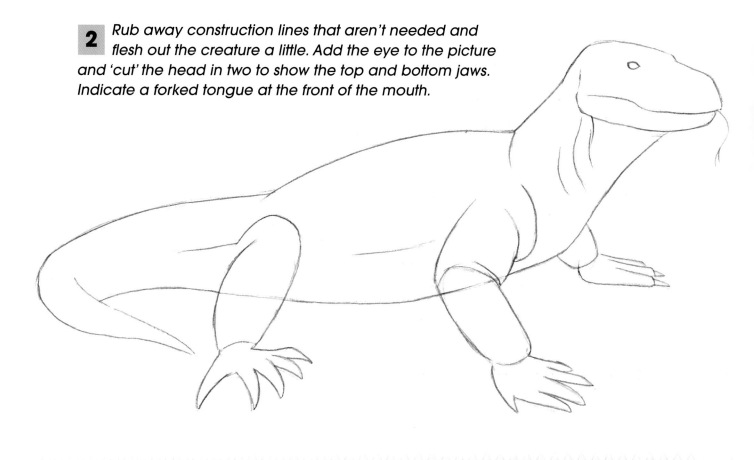

3 Use an HB pencil to put more detail into the drawing. Notice the details of the hands, feet and claws. Also draw in the skin folds. The komodo dragon has folds down its neck and along its back and body between the front and back legs.

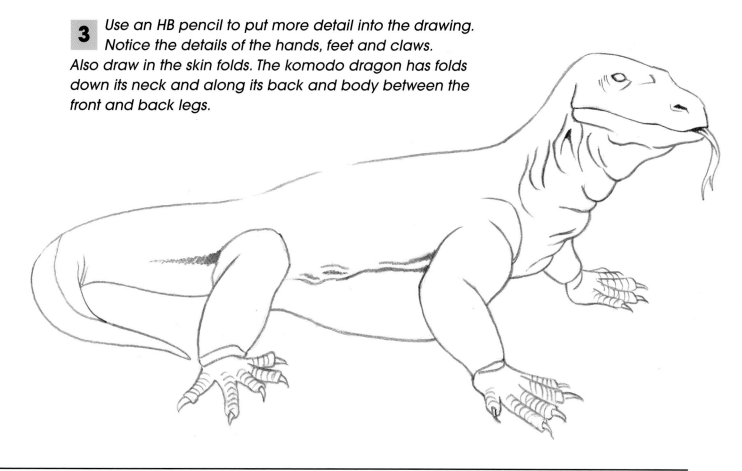

4 *Use a green and an orange pencil to add colour, as shown. Be careful not to colour in the areas on top of the head, legs and back. This is to be left white and will act as a highlight to show where light reflects off the creature. This will give the drawing a 3D effect.*

5 *Use a purple pencil and a sharp HB pencil to put extra detail into the markings. A darker pencil can also be used to darken up areas around the eye and on the feet.*

6 *Now add the details that will bring a touch of realism to this drawing. Add darker layers of colour to the underside of the body to create shadow. Notice the darkness and depth to the shadow just below the body on the ground. An orange pencil has been used to add further colour to the creature's back, head, neck and upper legs. A cross-hatching technique has been used all over the creature's body to add texture.*

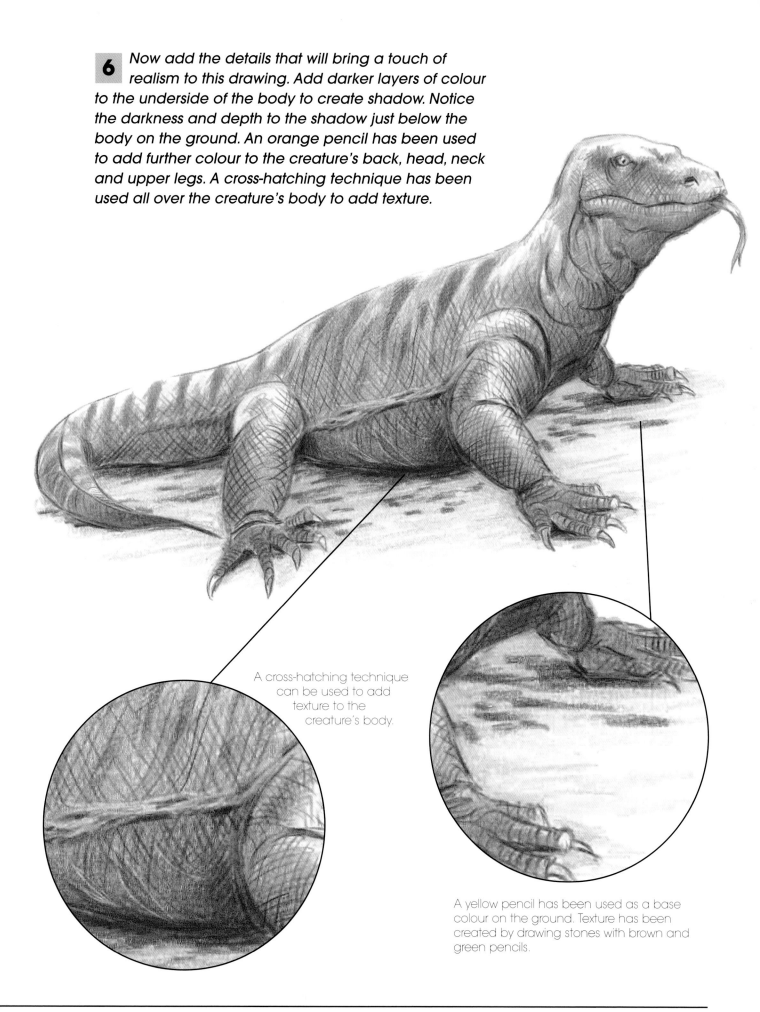

A cross-hatching technique can be used to add texture to the creature's body.

A yellow pencil has been used as a base colour on the ground. Texture has been created by drawing stones with brown and green pencils.

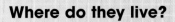

How to Draw

THAI WATER DRAGON

Thai water dragons are large lizards with a crest of teeth-like scales from neck to tail and a hump on their head. They live near water waiting to ambush prey, which comprises insects and small lizards. They have long back legs and a pinkish chin and neck.

Where do they live?

Water dragons can be found in south eastern Asia, China and India. They are found in tropical rainforests, usually close to a water source.

1 *Start by using a 3B pencil very lightly. Draw the head, body and tail of the water dragon and simply indicate where the legs come out of the body. Watch for proportions of the head and neck in relation to the body.*

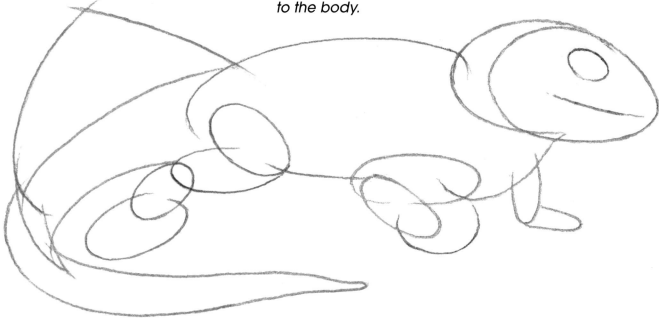

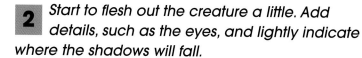

2 *Start to flesh out the creature a little. Add details, such as the eyes, and lightly indicate where the shadows will fall.*

3 *Now we can correct our drawing, filling in fine details. Look carefully at the beautiful scales on the throat. As always, lightly draw the scales first, gradually building up detail.*

4 *Use a green pencil to add colour to the face, neck, shoulders and back scales, as shown. Carefully add colour to the eye, leaving a white highlight at the centre of the pupil. Add purple colouring to the scales below the mouth.*

5 *Carefully bring colour to the rest of the drawing. Notice how the yellow pencil has been used to highlight the areas where light falls onto the creature. Browns, reds, yellows and black have been applied to the tail fin and really bring the creature to life.*

How to Draw

EMERALD TREE BOA

The emerald tree boa is fully adapted for life off the ground. Their intense green colour blends in perfectly with their leafy rainforest habitat. They prefer to live coiled-up on branches of trees that are near water, waiting, with their head hanging down, ready to strike at any passing birds and small mammals.

Where do they live?

Emerald tree boas are native to northern South America. They live in trees and bushes adjacent to water courses, swamps and marshes in rainforests.

1 *Start by lightly using a green pencil. Draw the head and body of the boa and simply indicate where the branch and leaves will be. When starting your base drawing, follow the loops of the creature through the body to ensure that each coil is in the correct position.*

2 Add more detail to your drawing. You can still rub out and correct anything that is incorrect. Look at the pattern of the scales on the head and body. Rub away lines that you don't need and flesh out the creature a little.

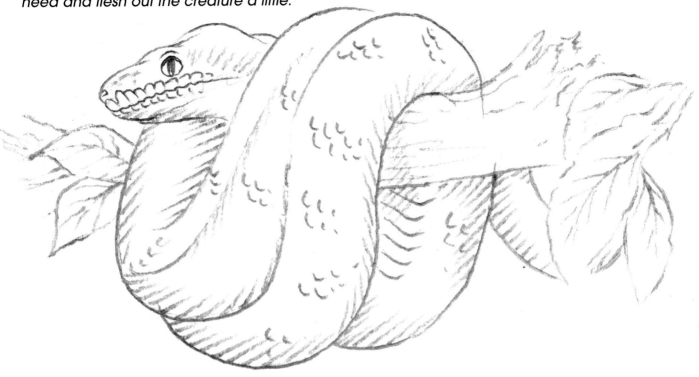

3 Tidy up your drawing using stronger lines. Add the eye to the picture and add more details around the mouth and leaves. When filling in detail, look at how the scales form the shape of the body.

Try drawing the scales on a spare piece of paper first to get the hang of them.

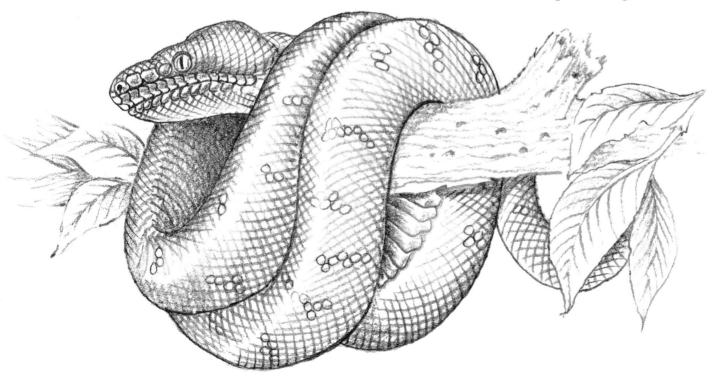

4 *Start by adding the lighter colours, gently building up the lovely green shade of the boa. Add yellow tints to the underside of the snake's body, to the eye and to the outer edges of the scales around the mouth.*

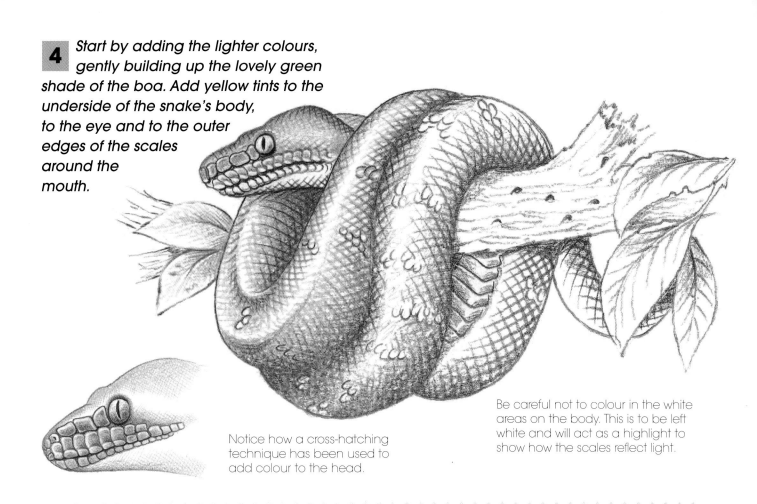

Notice how a cross-hatching technique has been used to add colour to the head.

Be careful not to colour in the white areas on the body. This is to be left white and will act as a highlight to show how the scales reflect light.

5 *Remember the loops and coils of the snake's body as you add more detail and colour. Follow along the lines to make sure they form the body properly.*

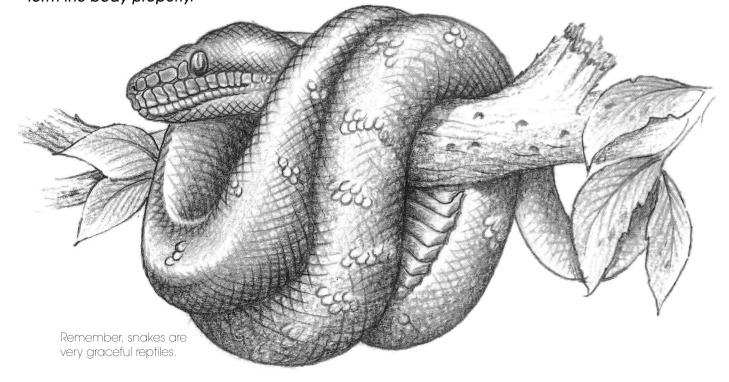

Remember, snakes are very graceful reptiles.

How to Draw

KING COBRA

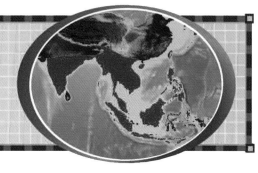

King cobras are the world's longest venomous snakes and their favourite food is other snakes. When threatened they raise the front third of their body so that they stand up to 1.3 m tall! Their venom is not as toxic as other cobras but they are dangerous to humans because they can inject a much larger amount of venom.

Where do they live?

King cobras live mainly in the rainforests and plains of India, southern China, and south east Asia.

1 When starting your base drawing, follow the loops of the creature through the body to ensure that each coil is in the correct position. The first sketch of the drawing should be done with a 3B pencil.

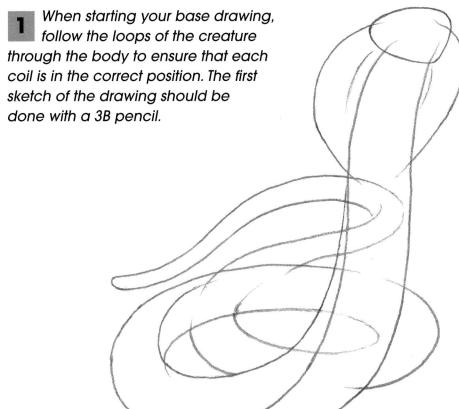

2 *Start to add detail to the drawing. Lightly indicate where shadows will fall and add leaves to the ground.*

3 *Continue to add more detail to your drawing. You can still rub out and correct anything that doesn't look quite right. Pay particular attention to the pattern of the scales on the head and extended hood.*

4 *Start adding light colour to the snake. Use brown and yellow pencils on the scales and use a red pencil to highlight the eyes and mouth.*

5 *Now you can add the deeper colours, giving form to the lovely coils. Gently add background to complement the animal. Use a black pencil to add depth to the gaps between the scales and to add shadow to the snake's underside.*

Check the position of the scales using the original guidelines.

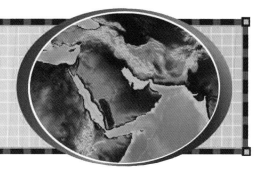

How to Draw

VEILED CHAMELEON

Veiled chameleons have a helmet-like ridge on top of their heads. This is a tiny swelling as a hatchling, but grows to 5 cm in height as the animal matures. They stalk their prey slowly, following it with eyes that can move independently and look in two directions at once, as well as swivel nearly 180 degrees! When prey is within range, they flick out their long, muscular tongue and catch the unsuspecting insect with the thick, sticky tip.

Where do they live?

Veiled chameleons are native to Yemen, United Arab Emirates and Saudi Arabia, and can be found in the dry plateaus, mountains and river valleys.

1 *Start by using a 3B pencil very lightly. Draw the head and body of the chameleon and simply indicate where the legs come out of the body and where the feet attach to the branch.*

This stage is purely to get a feel for the proportions and the position of the finished drawing.

2 When you are happy with the overall shape, change to an HB pencil and start adding a little detail. Put in the eye and crest on the head and draw in the individual toes. Flesh out the legs and fill out the branch on which the chameleon is walking.

3 At this stage use a putty rubber to take out any lines that aren't needed. The circles that indicate where the feet go can be erased and any lines inside the legs or body of the animal should be taken out too.

Add a little more detail – the markings on the body, mouth, nostril and the tiny spines under the chin and along the back.

4 Use a dark green pencil and a bright lime green pencil to add colour, as shown. Be careful not to colour in the areas on top of the head, legs and back. This is to be left white and will act as a highlight to give the drawing a 3D feel.

5 Use an orange and a yellow pencil to put extra detail into the markings. Use a purple or dark brown pencil to add scales on the crest and draw a criss-cross pattern on the body to show the reptilian skin. Keep the pencil sharp and draw lots of little circles around the head. This darker pencil can also be used to darken up areas around the eye and on the feet.

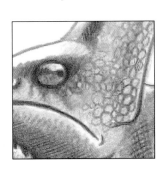

It is the little details, such as the scales on the head, that bring the picture to life and define areas of interest.

How to Draw

FRILLED LIZARD

These are truly spectacular lizards!
Their name derives from the large,
brightly coloured leathery frill around
their neck which opens up like an
umbrella when they are threatened. Frilled
lizards mainly forage on the ground for
termites and ants, which are the bulk of their diet,
and very occasionally feed on small mammals and lizards.

Where do they live?

Frilled lizards are found in tropical and warm
open woodland and savannah woodland in
southern New Guinea and northern Australia.

1 *Gently use your 3B pencil to draw the 3D outline of the frilled lizard. Indicate the dimensions of the creature and take care to ensure that the body proportions are correct.*

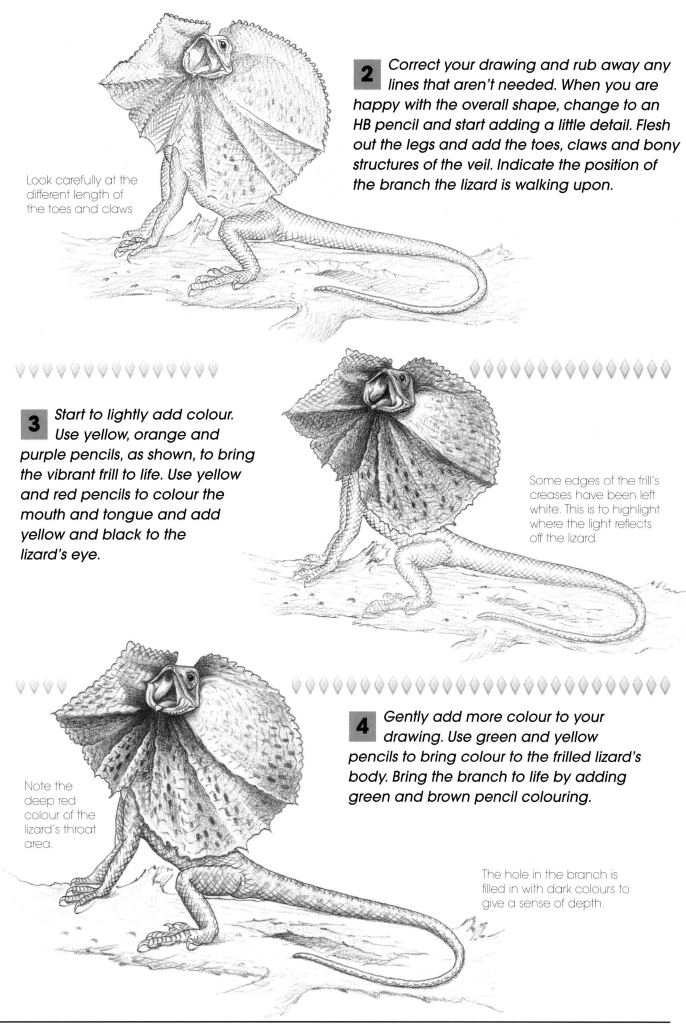

Look carefully at the different length of the toes and claws

2 Correct your drawing and rub away any lines that aren't needed. When you are happy with the overall shape, change to an HB pencil and start adding a little detail. Flesh out the legs and add the toes, claws and bony structures of the veil. Indicate the position of the branch the lizard is walking upon.

3 Start to lightly add colour. Use yellow, orange and purple pencils, as shown, to bring the vibrant frill to life. Use yellow and red pencils to colour the mouth and tongue and add yellow and black to the lizard's eye.

Some edges of the frill's creases have been left white. This is to highlight where the light reflects off the lizard.

Note the deep red colour of the lizard's throat area.

4 Gently add more colour to your drawing. Use green and yellow pencils to bring colour to the frilled lizard's body. Bring the branch to life by adding green and brown pencil colouring.

The hole in the branch is filled in with dark colours to give a sense of depth.

How to Draw

LEOPARD GECKO

Leopard geckos get their name from their patterned skin which resembles a leopard's coat. They have a thick tail which is used to store food. In times of plenty the tail increases in size, but it shrinks during droughts, when the surplus food is turned into energy. The tail may be discarded in defence, but not as readily as with other species of gecko.

Where do they live?

Leopard geckos are found in the deserts of southern central Asia including Iran, Iraq, Pakistan and western India. They live in warm areas where there are plenty of rocks for shelter.

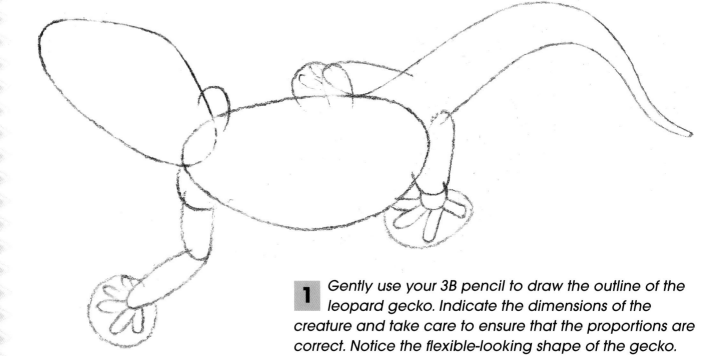

1 *Gently use your 3B pencil to draw the outline of the leopard gecko. Indicate the dimensions of the creature and take care to ensure that the proportions are correct. Notice the flexible-looking shape of the gecko.*

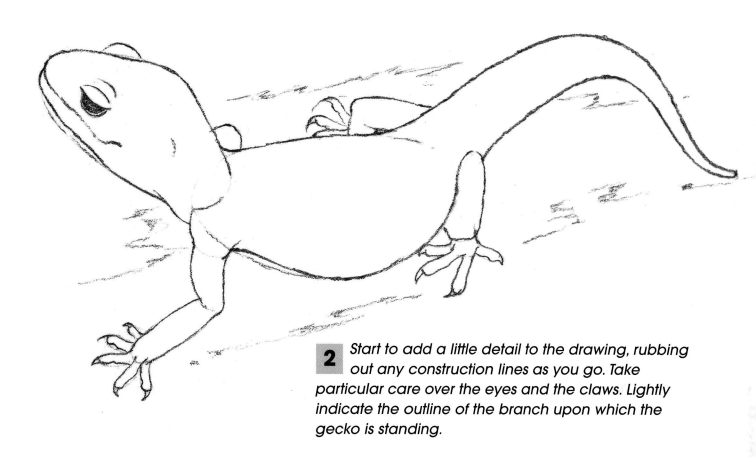

2 Start to add a little detail to the drawing, rubbing out any construction lines as you go. Take particular care over the eyes and the claws. Lightly indicate the outline of the branch upon which the gecko is standing.

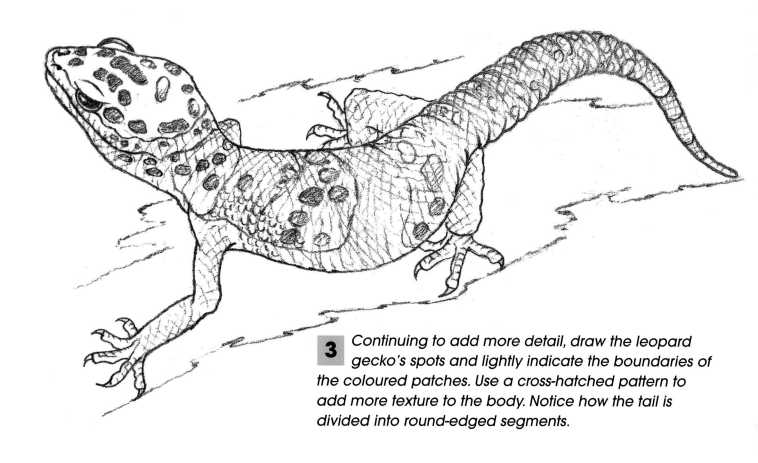

3 Continuing to add more detail, draw the leopard gecko's spots and lightly indicate the boundaries of the coloured patches. Use a cross-hatched pattern to add more texture to the body. Notice how the tail is divided into round-edged segments.

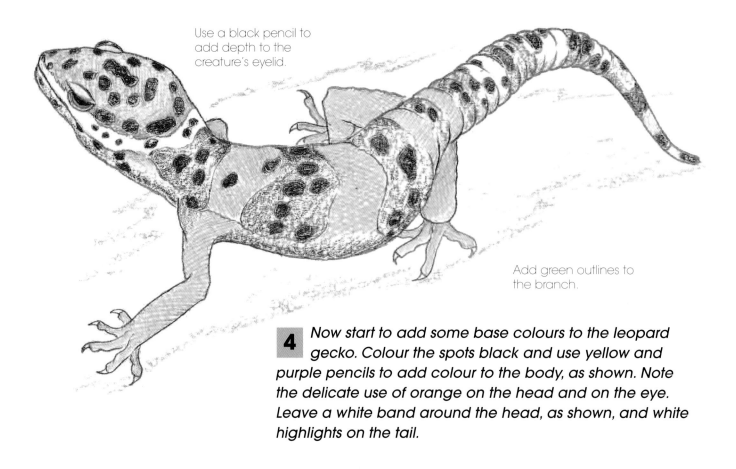

Use a black pencil to add depth to the creature's eyelid.

Add green outlines to the branch.

4 Now start to add some base colours to the leopard gecko. Colour the spots black and use yellow and purple pencils to add colour to the body, as shown. Note the delicate use of orange on the head and on the eye. Leave a white band around the head, as shown, and white highlights on the tail.

Add orange and green colouring to the branch.

5 Now it is time to add the details that will really bring this creature to life. Use a hard pencil to add many tiny circles to the drawing; these will give the impression of scaly skin. Draw cross-hatched patterns on the toes and legs with a red pencil and deepen the spots with a black pencil. Apply more colour to the tail, remembering to leave white highlights that will portray reflected light.

NILE CROCODILE

The Nile crocodile has long jaws, and you can see its teeth even when its mouth is closed. They have a dark olive to grey body with dark crossbands. The adults mainly eat fish but other prey may include zebras, hippos, porcupines, pangolins and migrating wildebeest, which are pulled into the water when they are drinking.

Where do they live?

Nile crocodiles are found throughout Africa and western Madagascar, in rivers, freshwater marshes, estuaries and mangrove swamps.

1 *Gently start to draw the creature's outline with a 3B pencil. Be careful to get the proportions of the mouth and tail correct and notice how the crocodile bulges around the belly and neck.*

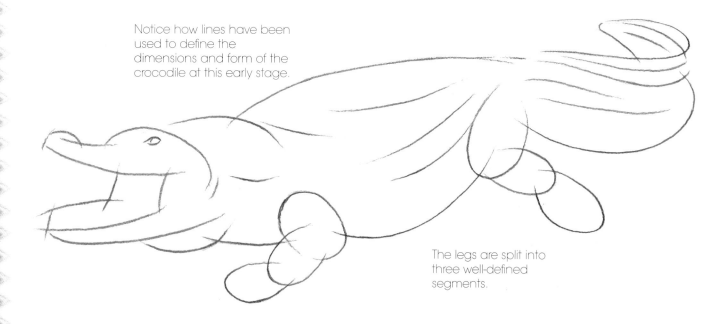

Notice how lines have been used to define the dimensions and form of the crocodile at this early stage.

The legs are split into three well-defined segments.

2 Start to flesh out the creature and rub away any construction lines that you don't need with an eraser. Gently add some light shading to the underside of the body, and to the back of the mouth, as a first layer of shadow. Draw some scales on the crocodile's back and neck and add teeth to the mouth.

Notice how the scales along the crocodile's tail are arrow shaped and sharp looking. The feet are slightly webbed and the claws sharp.

3 To add more detail to the drawing, continue to cover the crocodile with scales. Use a cross-hatching technique to add deeper shadowing to the underside of the crocodile's body and along the edges of the legs. Add more detail to the face and to the inside of the mouth.

Add some texture to the ground using darker shades to create the first layer of shadow.

4 *Use a dark orange pencil and a yellow coloured pencil to bring colour to the inside of the crocodile's mouth. Add a layer of yellow pencil to the crocodile's scales but leave the prominent edges with a white highlight. Build up the tone of the creature's skin with red, green and brown pencils.*

Darken the lines between the scales to add depth to the skin.

5 *Continue to darken the lines on the drawing and add more depth to the shadows. Remember to build up the colour and tones of the skin with yellow, green, brown, red, blue and purple pencils.*

Notice how the colour of the scales on the tail is a blend of red, green and blue. The edges of the raised scales have been left with a white highlight to show where light hits them.

How to Draw

AMERICAN ALLIGATOR

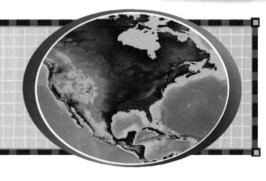

Large, powerful predators, American alligators are black with a broad head and rounded snout and have a heavily plated back. They feed in, or near, fresh water, preying on animals of all kinds, including birds snatched from low branches!

Where do they live?

American alligators are common in lakes, swamps and marshes of southeast USA.

1 *Start off by drawing a long slug shape leaving a slight bulge just behind the head. Add the legs, one pair just behind the neck and the other at the start of the tail.*

2 Draw in the front claws and add the long, slightly curved claws on the back leg. Add the eye to the picture and 'cut' the head in two to show the top and bottom jaws. Add a line to show where the back stops being flat and starts to curve around towards the belly.

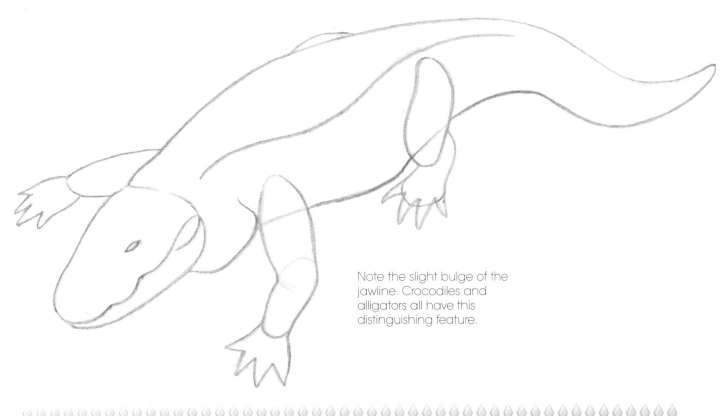

Note the slight bulge of the jawline. Crocodiles and alligators all have this distinguishing feature.

3 Continue to add detail to the drawing; notice the teeth coming from the top jaw and the bony ridges on top of the head behind the eyes. Also draw in the scales that the alligator has along its back and along the body between the front and back legs.

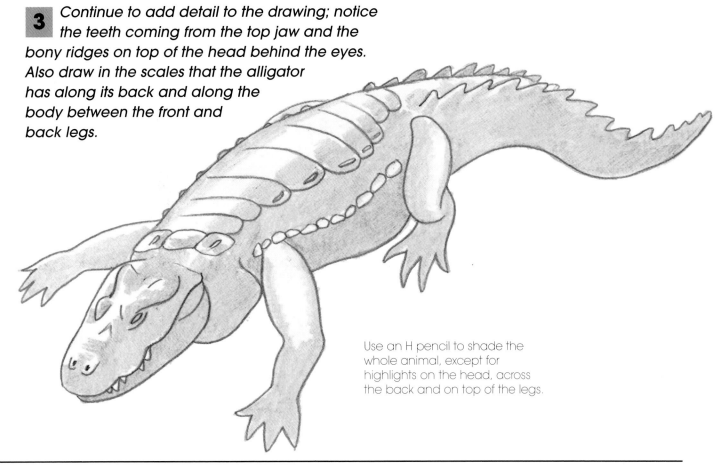

Use an H pencil to shade the whole animal, except for highlights on the head, across the back and on top of the legs.

4 Draw a criss-cross pattern across the legs and on the neck to give the appearance of scales. Try to draw the lines so that they follow the line of the animal – curving as the lines go underneath the body or around the legs. Use a B pencil to darken up the shadows at the base of the alligator. Build these tones up lightly and gradually merge each layer into the hard pencil tone.

On the lower scales of the legs try to leave the top surface of the scale white to show how the light catches the prominent edge.

5 The last stage is to darken up areas of interest with a 2B or 3B pencil – the area around the eyes, along the bottom of the belly, in the crevasses under the lower jaw and around the legs. Use a 2B pencil sharpened to a point to draw lots of little irregular circles across the body to create a scaled effect. The shadow the alligator casts on the ground is the last touch.

How to Draw

GALAPAGOS TORTOISE

The Galapagos tortoise is the biggest tortoise in the world! They spend most of their time grazing in small groups and basking in pools or mud wallows. They have strong toothless jaws that rip any tough vegetation they can feed on, including spiky cacti.

Where do they live?

These giant tortoises are found on the Galapagos islands, which lie west of Ecuador, on dry land with plenty of succulent plants to feed on.

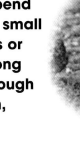

1 *Draw the loose outline of the tortoise with a 3B pencil. Keep in mind the proportions of the head, neck and legs in relation to the shell.*

2 *Rub away any lines you don't need and flesh out the creature a little by adding light shading to the legs and to the underside of the neck, body and shell. Draw in the feet and the toes.*

Add a few lines beneath the tortoise to represent the ground upon which the creature is walking.

3 *Continue to add detail to the drawing, tidying it up with stronger lines. Add scales to the tortoise's legs and wrinkles to the neck. Use darker shading to add depth to the shadows under the edges of the shell, to the gaps between the scales and to the wrinkles on the neck.*

Add more detail to the ground, including grass.

4 Use brown, green and blue pencils to lightly add colour to the creature's face. Note the delicate use of blue around the eye. Use a black pencil to add depth to the wrinkles on the creature's neck and between the scales on the leg.
You can still use your putty rubber to gently erase any lines you don't need.

Use a black pencil to bring the tortoise's eye to life, but leave a white highlight to indicate light reflecting from the eye.

5 Finish applying colour to the drawing, as shown. Notice how a purple pencil has been used to give the shell character. Continue to deepen the shadows to add shape and detail.

Notice the areas left white which act as a highlight to give the drawing a 3D feel. Continue to darken the shadows to give depth.

Count the toes and note their position.

How to Draw

ALLIGATOR SNAPPING TURTLE

These fearsome-looking animals are one of the world's largest freshwater turtles. They hunt during the day, mainly by sitting and waiting, and are equipped with a lure on their tongue that looks like a worm, to entice fish towards their scissor-sharp jaws. When prey gets too close, their hooked upper and lower beak deliver a powerful bite.

Where do they live?

Alligator snapping turtles are found in sloughs and deep muddy pools of large rivers in southeast USA. They are especially widespread in the lower Mississippi valley.

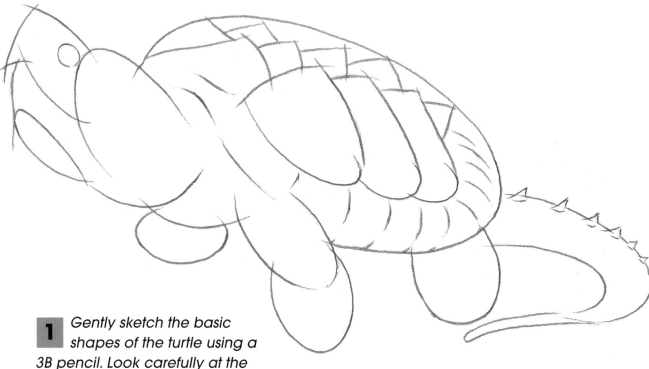

1 *Gently sketch the basic shapes of the turtle using a 3B pencil. Look carefully at the proportions of the head, shell, legs and tail.*

2 *Erase any lines you don't need and flesh out the creature a little by adding shading to the legs and to the underside of the head and tail. Draw more detail on the feet and the claws. Look carefully at the shell and note the number of sharp bumps.*

3 *Start to define more detail, remembering that you can still rub out lines if you are not happy. Use darker shading to add depth to the shadows between the shell plates and under the edges of the shell.*

Pay particular attention when adding texture and shape to the turtle's shell.

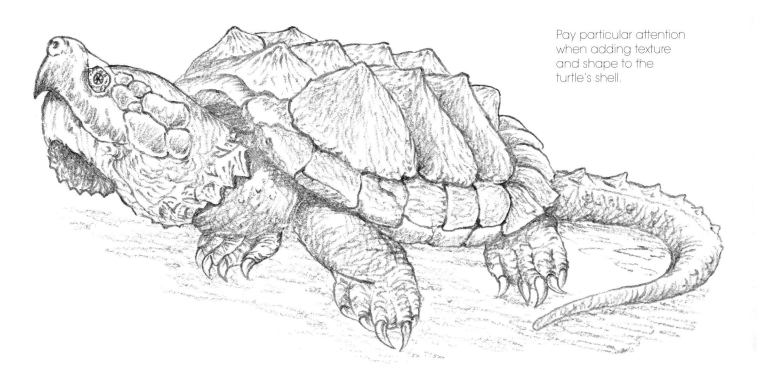

Add a white highlight to the eye to create a glint of light.

4 *Use brown, light brown, purple and green coloured pencils to lightly add colour to the turtle's head. Use yellow and black pencils to bring the turtle's eye to life.*

5 *Gradually add more colour to the turtle. Use green and brown pencils to bring colour to the shell and tail. Again, notice the prominent edges are left white, which acts as a highlight to give the drawing a 3D effect. Continue to deepen the shadows to give shape.*

Use the putty rubber to create paler highlights and further enhance the shape of the shell by adding deeper shadow.

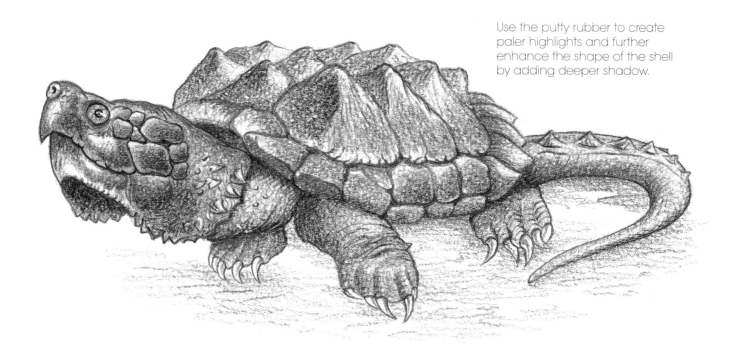

How to Draw

PTEROSAUR

Pterosaurs flourished between 150 million and 66 million years ago during the late Cretaceous period. They included the first, and largest, flying animals with backbones. While some were as small as canaries, others were as large as aeroplanes. Anhanguera, the creature to the right, had a 4-5 m wingspan and a large skull.

Where did they live?

Anhangueras lived 112 million years ago in what is now Brazil. They may also have lived over the ocean and hunted fish to survive.

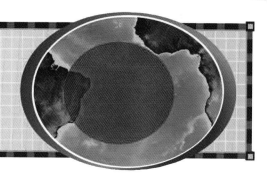

Notice the large shoulder muscles that would help to stabilise the wings in flight.

1 *A position at an angle works well for animals with large wingspans or long bodies. The large wing on the pterosaur's left shows the width of the wing, but the right wing is seen head on so appears very thin.*

2 Rub away any lines you don't need, flesh out the legs a little and add the toes and the tail. Add the bony structures that look like semicircles at the end of the jaw on this pterosaur.

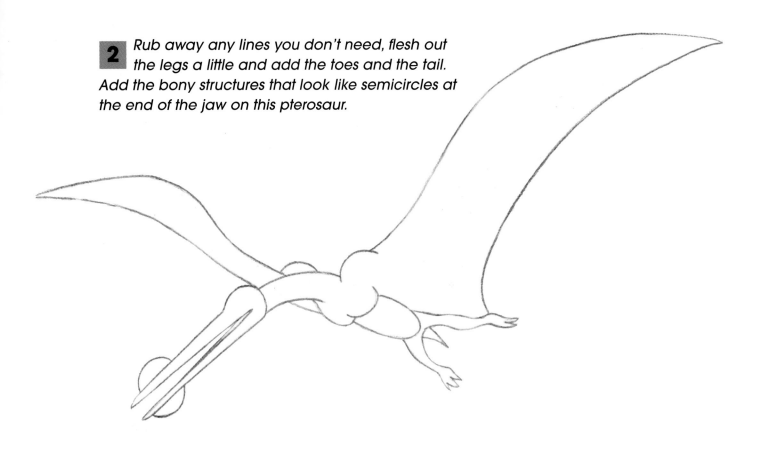

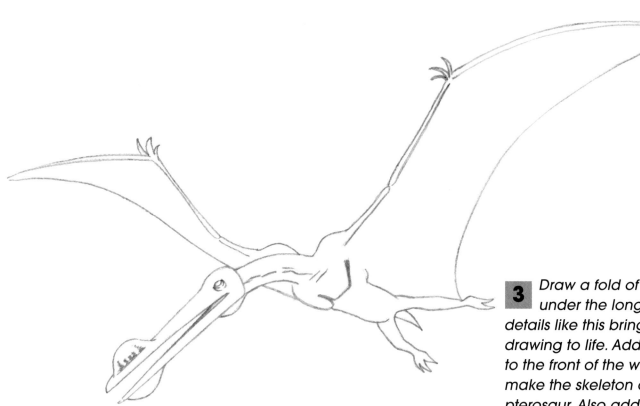

3 Draw a fold of skin under the long neck – details like this bring the drawing to life. Add the line to the front of the wings to make the skeleton of the pterosaur. Also add small claws at the leading edge of each wing.

4 Shade the whole creature with a small pencil leaving a few highlights on the head and shoulder muscles to make these look rounded. Try to keep the tone even all over the body.

Make the pterosaur look reptilian by adding lots of little lines across the legs and claws. This creates a scaled effect.

5 Begin to shade over the pale grey, with darker shades of pencil, to bring out shadows on the wing, on the underside of the neck and lower jaw. Darken up the area around the eye and note the triangular shapes on the jaw where the teeth come from. Draw these in as well as the nostrils and the earholes.

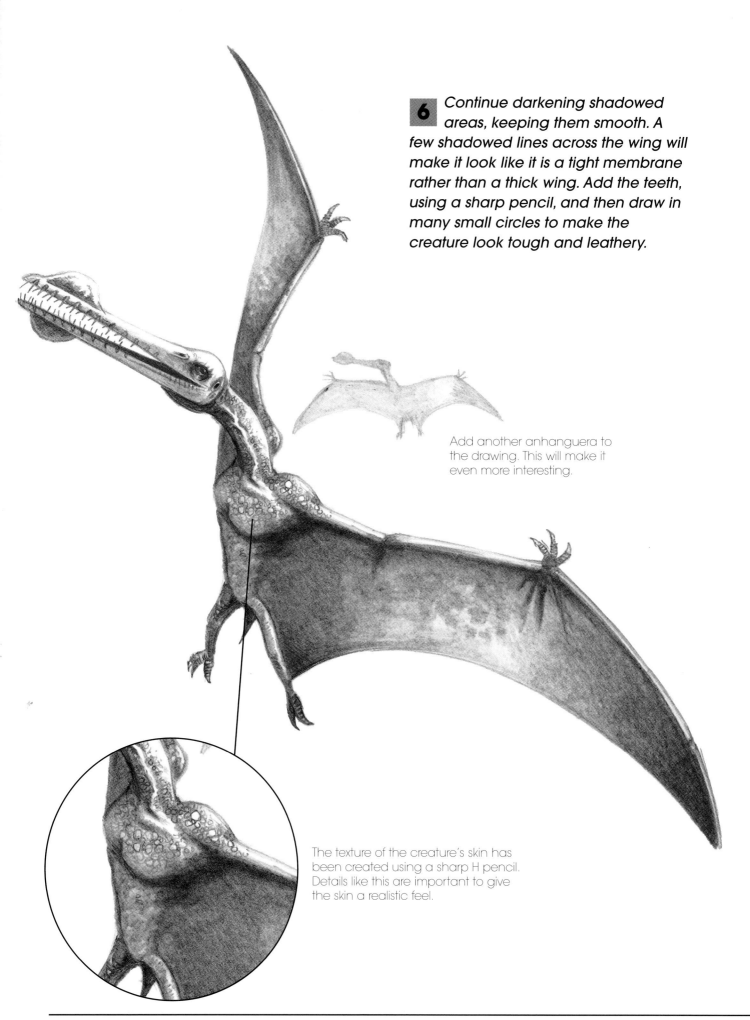

6 Continue darkening shadowed areas, keeping them smooth. A few shadowed lines across the wing will make it look like it is a tight membrane rather than a thick wing. Add the teeth, using a sharp pencil, and then draw in many small circles to make the creature look tough and leathery.

Add another anhanguera to the drawing. This will make it even more interesting.

The texture of the creature's skin has been created using a sharp H pencil. Details like this are important to give the skin a realistic feel.

How to Draw

MASTERCLASS DRAWINGS

Every artist starts as a beginner. The difference between a poor artist and a good one is a matter of observation, practice, and learning from other artworks. In the same way, every picture starts as a basic sketch. These few pages will show you how to compose a drawing or painting, and how to learn to look at things to see them as they really are.

OBSERVATION AND SKETCHING

The best way to learn how things look is to take a sketch book to the zoo, and practise rough sketches of the different reptiles you see. Study the way their bodies are put together and the different textures of their skin and scales.

Draw the rough outline first, using simple shapes as you have learnt to capture the proportions of the creature. Add more detail to this to pinpoint where the main features are. If you're sketching roughs to work on at home, make sure you've got the detail you need to finish the picture.

Slow-moving creatures, like crocodiles, are good to start with. You can take your time over the sketch without them altering position. Faster animals, like lizards, are a new challenge. You'll have to learn to capture the main body shape quickly, before they move.

TAKING NOTES

When you're sketching, your aim is to capture enough detail to allow you to draw a completed picture at home. Make colour notes as you sketch, or use coloured pencils in small areas to remind you of colour differences. Your main sketching tool, however, is your pencil.

1 *Make sketch notes of anything you find interesting or unusual about the creature. In particular, sketch anything that you didn't realise about the animal. Maybe you'd never noticed the pattern of its scales, for example, or the way its mouth is shaped.*

2 *Draw some background detail to remind yourself of the size of your main subject. If you're putting the animal against a background, you'll need to know how big it is. Food, or other animals, will remind you of the scale to work to.*

The sketch (below) has been used later as a reference for a more detailed drawing (bottom left).

3 *What you leave off is as important as the marks you make on the paper. Look at the sketch here (far right). There is very little colour or pencil work in the highlights – the areas which are catching the most light.*

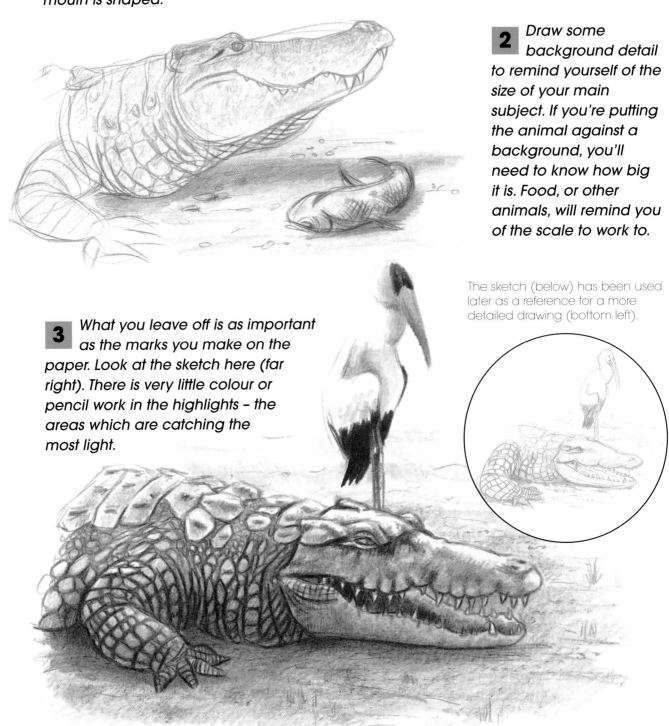

BACK AT HOME

With your sketches in front of you, you can decide in which position you want to draw your animal. Don't panic if you have left some vital detail off your sketch. Photographs can be really helpful to fill in any gaps. Look in books, or on the internet, and you should find plenty of examples of your chosen animal. They will help you to study colours, textures and any other details your sketch may be lacking.

1 *Photos can also be a good way to start sketching. Try to see the hidden shapes, as shown in the step-by-steps throughout this book. Learn to take the leap from looking at your animal, straight to sketching their body shape, without having to draw in the basic shapes first.*

2 *Use photos when you're drawing to check that you have the right shades and hues. It's a great way to really focus in on some of the creature's finer details.*

SETTING THE SCENE

You may be happy with your crocodile on its own, but the chances are you'll want to add something in the background. Experiment with different styles. Some pictures look great with other animals behind them, while others look better with simple backgrounds, like a patch of stony ground.

In this example, the main crocodile is joined by another one. They have both been set against a natural background of foliage and scenery. The scenery adds depth to the picture, making it a better 3D representation.

Study the background as you draw, just the way you've learnt to do with your reptiles. Look carefully at the areas of light and shadow. Notice also the way that tones are more distinct in the foreground, and fainter the further back you go.

WHEN IS A DRAWING FINISHED?

Don't overwork your pictures. Learn to see when you've done enough to create impact, without making your picture too busy or crowded. It's also important to learn that you can stop when you've had enough. Drawing is done for pleasure, so you don't have to keep working at it until you're fed up. Having said that, it's more likely that you'll get engrossed in your work and never want to stop!

Picture Credits

NHPA
Nature P1